BEYOND

Sarah Wardle was born in London in 1969, and studied Classics at Oxford, and English at Sussex, where she gained her doctorate. In 1999 she won the Geoffrey Dearmer Prize, *Poetry Review*'s new poet of the year award. Her first book, *Fields Away* (Bloodaxe Books, 2003), was shortlisted for Forward Best First Collection, and was followed by *Score!* (2005), *A Knowable World* (2009) and *Beyond* (2014), all from Bloodaxe. She has been poet-in-residence for Bedgbury National Pinetum, Tottenham Hotspur Football Club, the British Council in Berlin and Transport for London at Embankment Station, and Royal Literary Fund Fellow at Royal Holloway, is a poetry lecturer at Morley College, Lecturer in Poetry at Middlesex University, and a FRSA.

SARAH WARDLE

BEYOND

BLOODAXE BOOKS

ISBN: 978 1 78037 097 2

First published 2014 by
Bloodaxe Books Ltd,
Highgreen,
Tarset,
Northumberland NE48 1RP.

www.bloodaxebooks.com
For further information about Bloodaxe titles
please visit our website or write to
the above address for a catalogue.

Supported by
**ARTS COUNCIL
ENGLAND**

Cover design: Neil Astley & Pamela Robertson-Pearce.

Printed in Great Britain by Bell & Bain Limited, Glasgow, Scotland, on
acid-free paper sourced from mills with FSC chain of custody certification.

Let London be a city of love
beyond its competition and isolation!
Sun and moon, keep watch from above
on each Thames-dweller at every tide, bridge and station!
Shepherds of the sky, look out for our town!
Build us up with hope when we're falling down!

ACKNOWLEDGEMENTS

Acknowledgements are due to the following publications in which some of these poems first appeared: *Poetry Review* ('Keeping Going', 'Chinese Calligraphy', 'Single', 'Full English', 'Freeman'), *South Bank Poetry* ('The Listeners'), *The Spectator* ('Night Watch', 'Finding', 'On Lambeth Bridge', 'The Passage') and *The Times Literary Supplement* ('Country Life', 'Management Logic', 'Twelfth Night', 'Drift', 'Freshers', 'National Speed Limit').

'Give' appeared on the website of NBFA Assisting the Elderly.

CONTENTS

Beyond

(for Constance Wardle, 1905-2006)

Because one day the ocean's cold abyss,
which roars without knowing it is heard
for it was sound before there was a word,
will sweep us to a place where nothing is,

and because, while we live, we sail alone,
may all of us keep each of us in mind
beyond this world, beyond the ends of time,
to give us hope as we travel the road,

as on the morning after you had died
you gave me strength to follow the horizon
even to the end in no direction,
as you spoke through winter sun and sky,

or like that day of snow when, glad to exist,
I saw a goose foraging in white
and was filled with the togetherness of life
and wanted not just to be, but to persist.

Chinese Calligraphy

Music is the same character as happiness.
Upright is like, but not the same as, heaven,
which with some alteration turns to peace.

For some reason the past looks like yellow,
while eternity is similar to source
and city reminiscent of purple.

A book seems related to the end.
Safe and dark could easily be confused.
Heart needs more strokes to make it forget.

Watching a Ta'ziye

Here the faces of the crowd are one,
from singular to plural, private to universal.
They move across the camera like clouds,
or changeable weather,
as if we're watching a medieval passion play.
No need for translation.
This martyrdom is like the crucifixion.

Waves of emotion transliterate grief
on a child's face.
Are these the men of ancient Athens
watching Oedipus, Orestes?
It's quiet, but for tears
and the songs and calls of actors.
This martyrdom is a reflection.

Here truth is light in refraction.
I'm one of the spectators of the installation,
of those who watched the pageant in Iran.
This is religion and showmanship,
not indoors like the Vatican does it,
but out in an open air arena,
cathartic as Greek theatre.

This is the interface of film and performance.
I see the gaze of spectators as they watch.
The crowd are like people in grief,
and here in this auditorium
we become imitations,
copies of the original audience
with their emotional response.

We read the play through their faces.
There is silent music in their expressions,
sincere as symphonies.
An audience within the film
is screened to further audiences.
That boy, this woman, that old man
comfort and console, conjoin and mourn.

Beyond the Ends of Time

As I grow older I think less and less
of the world according to Heraclitus,
that all is in flux and nothing remains.
More and more I incline to Larkin's
view that what remains of us is love,
though I find it ever harder to prove.
For if, like him, I leave no son, or daughter,
then there'd not be even Heraclitean water.
Rather than flowing on, it'd evaporate.
Perhaps what lasts is love, what dies is hate.
So maybe there is something that stands still,
an outlook of good nature and goodwill,
a stillness of body and of mind
that we tap into in love, or when we're kind,
which are different, as kindness born of stillness
is deeper than the love that comes from madness,
though one, I think, can lead into the other,
in fact just like a Heraclitean river,
so possibly Zeno's paradox
defines the point where love rests and life stops,
and ice is the image that conjoins them,
the point of death and of lack of motion.
Then may my love for you be like the winter
at true and magnetic north. Long may it capture
the splinter through my heart, the icicle
of warmth, the dagger's stab of love's goodwill,
a snow diamond beyond melting's temperature,
a love that cannot change, will never thaw,
so even in the darkest entropy
what will survive in stillness is the plea
of kindness, the white flag of armistice,
the sense of peace and truce met in the kiss
of love which will outlast the universe.

Beyond Metaphysics

What is knowledge and what do we learn?
Epistemology, logic, proof of friends,
how to love and lose, essay and win
and that winning itself is not the end?

So is the metaphysical beyond,
or within, in jump of heart and mind,
in dragonfly and dawn breeze on a millpond,
sunlit wheat fields, acts of being kind,

in waves, like days, on continents and islands,
justice in action, burns becoming firths,
in the sense, not sign, of holding hands,
that truth is fact and loyalty, deaths and births,

that freedom from and to and human rights,
where dictators fill begging bowls and kill,
are not textbook examples, but real life
for leaders, governments, rebels, peoples?

Kitchen Garden

My aim is to make life as orderly
as rows of cabbages and lettuce,
make it yield a field of strawberries,
turn up pride like new potatoes,
grow plans into a prize marrow,
reap rewards like carrots from seed,
take despair as if it were manure,
use dissatisfaction like peat,
harvest runner beans of effort,
make care pay sweet-pea dividends,
launch my produce at the village fête,
pour libations to it with friends,
pare and boil and roast and share,
pickle as if in jars to savour.

Field Work

If you reckon days by dusks and dawns,
by upright forests and flat horizons,
you'll know truth is present in all things,
that we march with, or against, prevailing winds.

If you stride fast in a decreasing spiral,
or halt in the centre of a stone circle,
you'll know world is linked, driftwood to shell,
from a camp fire to a watchful eagle.

If you travel the path from fresh to salt water,
storm cloud to rainbow, mountain to shore,
you'll know you're more than a reflection in a river,
that you are circumference and diameter.

If you make ripples with splashes of stones,
the here-and-now becoming there-and-then,
you'll know after death we're remembered by friends
and that is how our souls can remain.

If you listen to the heart's rhythm of your tread,
the tidal ebb and flood, the flood and ebb,
you'll know you sew a line you'll never unthread,
as life's material becomes embroidered.

If you leave words in your wake, like a poet,
just as stepping stones have left you a gift,
and do not ask who or why, but how and if,
the universe will know you and you'll know it.

Night Music

Pray for all the deserts in the city,
where oases of hope are rarely found,
for prisoners, prostitutes, the pitied
homeless, destitute old, the underground

of London, the drunk, the mad, the addicts,
in whose veins a polluted river flows,
for asylum-seekers escaping the barbaric,
for those in pain, especially for those.

What happens inside rooms that glow at night?
Cocaine, violence, loneliness, abuse?
Who's dialling 999 after a fight?
Who's dying in that speeding ambulance?

That bottle breaking outside in the street,
those shouts from fans after their team has won,
that police siren, that couple's argument:
these are the lullaby of London town.

Listen. Rain is singing a litany
for all the lives that look as though they're lost.
A storm's echoing the insanity
from palaces and bars to tower blocks.

This city is paved with dog-shit, not gold.
Its skyline never sleeps to chase a dream.
Its hearts are overpriced, and bought and sold.
Its desires accelerate like engines.

The battered child crying himself to sleep,
the heroin-user shooting his fix,
the troubled woman jumping into the street,
will be ferried not on the Thames, but Styx.

Night Watch

The social worker says that blue sky thinking
is better than Beckett. In the daytime I agree,
but at night I think of those in cells, those drinking,
in pain, at war, on streets. It's hard to feel
hope at this hour, though I'm not in discomfort.
I'm clothed, fed, sheltered, trying to distract
myself, like a mother with an infant,
from the presence of a lack of human contact.
Across the street a lamp's on at a window.
Someone else postpones going to bed,
perhaps to work on something for tomorrow,
or else to silence thoughts inside his head.
The newspapers are full of suicides,
people who didn't make it to first light.

The Listeners

You might not know the city's solitude,
nights it feels like oblivion,
even when among a multitude
how it seems those millions are gone,
and because you are not in any pain,
sense no cold, no hunger and no thirst,
but for the sound of falling rain
(which since you hear, you are), you'd not exist,
until a sudden siren rends the dark,
sends hope and help in insistent heartbeats,
jolts you into being, brings you sharp
back to the contingent, where relief meets
a cardiac arrest, fire, or domestic,
strings lonely Londoners listening in bedsits.

City Walk

When the day is grey as pencil lead,
and sky on the verge of sieving rain,
and your mind soaked but still stained,
and work and love life both snagged,
when hope slips from your hands like soap,
and fertility is boiling dry,
and friendship fading like a dye,
and youth sinking like a bad joke,
let impulse move you to your feet,
throw on your coat, open the door,
experience the dark and downpour,
go forth and pace the city streets,
look through lit windows at lives like yours,
some better off, some far worse.

Midwinter

Faint-setting sun, red as a falling leaf,
when you have gone, it takes an act of faith
to know you are still up there in the sky
for as you disappear, it seems you die,
just as at the dark side of the moon
it looks as if Selene has been taken,
or just as when the moon is snowfall full,
it seems the stars are hardly there at all.
Yet your light reappears each morning,
heralded by the hyacinth pink of spring,
seeping watercolour across the horizon
until narcissus yellow follows on
and you rise even at the winter solstice,
promising midsummer's radiance.

Twelfth Night

My mother is sleeping,
which is to say recuperating
after her operation to remove death.

Her chest rises and falls,
like a small craft on the tide.
The Christmas tree is stripped bare.

This afternoon it snowed repeatedly.
We wait for the leaf's green,
for spring to unfurl.

Drift

Each day we move a step nearer loss
on treadmills we walk until we also die
with no comprehension of our purpose,
but that it is forbidden not to try
to keep going through snow, illness, grief.
That London links us is a consolation.
This morning Osbert Street was full of promise
that later you'd be here, though I'd be gone,
and on my return this evening to the square
I breathed the thoughts you left on icy air.

Keeping Going

Dawn spills relief after a long night. On a sill
hyacinths greet white sky. Now Big Ben
is striking seven o'clock and the streetlamps

die together with stairwell lights in the council
high-rise and a bulb above the No Entry sign.
I feel like a Fresher returning from the river,

where I caught a crab while I watched
the swans, my Latin prose still not yet done
for a tutorial at half-past nine. And you

don't need anti-depressants. Morning
sun is enough, the pace of eight o'clock
pavements, the urgency of Victoria station,

fifteen minutes at a coffee stand, a blue
sky high enough to dream into, the sharp
air of a January platform, frosted fields

seen from a train, a walk uphill, a face
you know, even just as an acquaintance,
a shared joke, shoots at an office window.

Festival of the Trees

Today is the Festival of the Trees
according to Abigail.
In Israel almond blossom is in flower,
but in Britain we have snow.

This morning Abi planted a tree
with the Pinner kindergarten.
There is still time for children.
We look to the trees.

Credo

The air is milder. Perhaps snow is past.
Dawn breaks earlier with every day.
Something in me says begin to trust,
even if I'm not the type to pray.
Daffodil stems are pushing through the earth
out of hibernation, longing for sun.
People are sensing suspension of hurt.
March is almost here, renewal begun.
How many more dark winters shall I face?
Will I yet bear a child in a kind of spring?
I won't chase life, but go at its own pace,
keeping an eye out for what it may bring,
glad for mornings the sky is blue and clear,
that evenings are for now but metaphor.

Commuters' Pentameter

Where are you in this surging crowd?
Are you a separate body, or part
of the Leviathan, the lungs, the heart?
Can you hear yourself think out loud,
or are you suffocating in the throng
that marches down The Strand as one,
stringing along the soul of London?
Were you given a choice to belong?
Should there be an opt-out clause
for those who don't want to be confirmed
into the mysteries citizens learn,
or are these more a blessing than a curse?
Is there solace in the rhythmic beat
that bears you on with iambic feet?

Citybreak

Sunlight is falling upon stone,
empires over, but the day begun.
Dawn ascends bridge, statue, dome
in Athens, Rome, Paris, London.
Crowds populate roads and days.
Politicians contend with the wise.
History follows its own ways.
The trees' green shoots are alive.
Life is a rush hour moving beyond
the courtesy of humanity.
Each capital fulfils its daily round
in office, home, theatre, park and street.
People cheer. Leaders steer and wave.
The sun represents the highest octave.

Breakfast Soliloquy

The washing machine echoes my soul,
getting in a spin, emotional,
unlike the cool composure
of this quietly processing computer.
A plane complains. A phone calls.
A drill whines. A bell warns.
Cars utter tenacity and drive.
Across the way a baby cries.
And is life the power behind the light?
Will spirit too shut down at night?
Is the ghost in the machine
the cursor's heartbeat on the screen?
Does the vacuum cleaner's hunger
voice our love for one another?

Rural Calm in the City Centre

As I look out to right and left, I am met by the red brick wall
of an office block that this morning, Saturday, is empty
of the men in suits who meet for trapped discussions
every weekday, no longer in rooms above with blinds down,
hiding them from view, or, when lit up, slicing them into
screened images. From the sofa I can see sky on the corner,
the summer green of a tall London plane, the Victorian house
at the end of the square, not bombed in the war. Nothing
is going on outside, and that is the point: how peaceful it is
at weekends without the proximity of people,
noise, cab drivers, civil servants, pedestrians.
And this Bank Holiday weekend, a triple-word-score silence
descends with Q for quiet, question, Z for zone.

Single

As your carriage slows past terraced houses,
where prices push up through paving cracks
and families along with the clothes on their backs
are hung out to dry like socks and blouses,
while children's bikes in gardens glimmer,
dying on their sides in spun-out silence,
wheels running down like a bank balance,
or the last hot days of summer,

and in rooms like stage sets saucepans simmer
to boiling point, while double beds at night
lie facing the walls, it's each blue light
that draws you in, tellies that flicker
like gas flames, glimpsed through open windows,
keeping campfires burning as wives
and husbands sit down to other lives,
like dreams, or their pale shadows,

and you know the theme tune is starting now,
drifting over rooftops like smoke, a strain
of notes like water gurgling down a drain,
that scenes will play, though they don't know how,
whether an adulterer will leave his wife,
whether a man will pay off his debts,
and they don't know if they're taking bets
on a television programme, or real life,

nor is it clear how your story will end,
what you should do, or what you can choose,
but you realise there's no plot to lose,
no other author on whom your scripts depend,
and as the train starts to pick up speed,
you're glad to be leaving the city behind
and your outlook broadens until you find
you've a widescreen view of fields and trees.

Full English

All around in the hotel
small talk of retired couples
is what the garrulous groom
signs up to this afternoon.
When he and his bride are old
and don't fit their photo clothes,
when their kids have fled the nest,
this will be their wedding breakfast.
As their hair turns the grey
of the rain that's on its way,
intimacy will reduce
to talk of toast and orange juice.
If they're lucky, years will prove
the ordinariness of love.

Progress

They are about to sacrifice to the goddess.
The calf knows its fate and stalls,
has to be pulled on a rope,

while young girls with flowers in their hair
follow behind, eyeing up the priests.
The matrons bear a woven cloth,

which has taken them four years to make
and will adorn the virgin's statue,
all in gold and larger than life.

Philosophers and historians observe
the spectacle with detached scepticism.
The tragedians on the other hand take part.

The people want to appease the goddess,
as only she can stop the war and plague.
They sing to their protector, as they process.

Outside the walls, the enemy advances,
laying waste the crops. At the same time,
hostile ships set sail for the harbour.

Watch how the rain starts and dim clouds
begin to stir up the blood-dark sea.
The calf lows. The young girls look away.

Now it seems as if civilisation were in vain.
And there, hard by the Acropolis,
just as the calf dies and the Spartans come,

spot the trader, selling red clay vases
with images of the gods throwing spears.
His kind will see the city rises from ruins.

Hope

(after George Frederic Watts)

Who did this to you, blindfolded your beauty,
left you alone on a spinning world
with no one to listen to your music,
a muse with a broken heart and lyre?
Is this what Zeus did after he had used you,
changed you by metamorphosis
from cheerleader to singer of the blues,
from freethinker to imprisoned pessimist?
Who said you were not good enough for him,
not pretty, young, intelligent and slim?
What man did this, stealing your self-belief?
Or is the truth you did this to yourself?
Your hands are untied. Let in the light!
No more melancholy. Sing of life!

On Lambeth Bridge

I am halfway across a bridge
and midway through my life,
staring at the midday sun.
How I love politics!
I recall hearing debates
over there in the Commons

and I know that democracy
is about working days like this,
taxpayers in trucks and buses,
the business of pleasure boats,
foreign policy of tourists
and waiting lists in St Thomas's,

and as the Eye revolves
like economic cycles,
the nation's travelled full circle
and the distance seems to widen
between Lambeth Palace
and the Square Mile,

and upstream MI6
runs information espionage,
while joggers run past
dog-walkers and mothers
with love's child benefit
in Battersea Park,

and Big Ben strikes the hour,
deploying anaphora,
rhetorically insistent,
as cold winds of change
deliver education
to a hardened electorate.

The Passage

Here the homeless queue
for motherly nuns
to dish out meat and veg,

for showers, clothes,
central heating,
company, conversation,

medical attention,
to use computers
to apply for jobs,

to borrow blankets against the cold,
suits for interviews,
an address for housing waiting lists:

economic migrants,
demobbed soldiers, the divorced,
mad, alcoholic, unemployed, unlucky

from Africa, Greece, Ireland,
Manchester, shop doorways
and Westminster Cathedral's steps.

Freshers

Now as the leaves fall, the Freshers come,
slim as saplings, every year so young,
embarking on their quest for a degree
of intellect and sex. You almost see
your cohort of nineteen-eighty-seven
among those who hadn't then been born.

They note what we say in lectures,
come for tutorials seeking answers
on how to be better, how to compete.
I want to tell them it's a dead heat,
that they're all in first place, beyond our reach,
and have what we can only teach.

Management Logic

It is May and I am marking
poems about the deaths of fathers,
Royal Marines, anorexia,
essays on contemporary fiction and drama,
year-long projects, work placement reports,
distinguishing upper from lower seconds
on shows of analysis and individuality.
The university has just axed Philosophy.
Thought still hangs deep in the green trees.
There is a protest banner which reads:
'Those who lack imagination
cannot imagine what is lacking.'
Students have occupied the Mansion Building.

Dairy Farm

Sometimes when a class reaches a close,
students come up to ask you to repeat
a deadline, or for handouts from last week,
as if they were a herd of curious cows,

big-eyed and in the summer of their lives,
backing you against a field gate,
saying sorry they, or their work, were late.
They graduate like cattle in black and white.

Awayday

As if all aboard a school coach
heading for an away match,
applauding talks as though singing
in solidarity like we're winning,

we congratulate our innovation
in interdisciplinary education,
where the researcher is practitioner
of adventures in knowledge transfer,

and students achieve learning outcomes
in diverse and plural forms,
project-based and for vocations,
enabling skills and dissemination

through multimedia communication,
experimentation and investigation,
where plural interests inform the syllabus,
and examination is active and curious,

leading us not only into inquiry,
but delivering us via discovery
of culture, processes and systems,
facilitating fresh observations,

where everything is interrelated
and originality validated
by the due deadline date.
Questions? Coffee? Comfort break?

National Speed Limit

The day you win the prize, or get the job,
always feels like that first school-bop snog,
or this stepping hard on the gas
with the radio turned up full blast,
no one else in sight on the road,
evening and summer not yet over,
the chorus kicking in like cannon fire,
the way ahead seemingly straight for ever.

Country Life

It is peace that strikes
even by the war memorial,
as if the umpire on the cricket green,
all dressed in white,
has saved the village
from the black-frocked vicar,
whose dirge at Christmas and Easter
heralds the euphoria
of exiting the church.
Here there are no police,
no ambulances, no fire engines,
no teeming streets.
You can see for miles into the distance,
fields and trees and hedgerows,
not another house in sight.

The Doctor

(after Sir Luke Fildes)

In the cottage dawn hope flickers
across her child's face like fanning embers.
This is what I've waited all night to find.

Her mother sent for me to cure her daughter.
How could I tell her she might not recover?
The worst part of my work is being unkind.

I walked here over three fields and a river.
Outside it is the middle of winter.
Inside we are trying to stave off time.

My wife will soon be going into labour.
These parents also tend her brothers and sister.
However much we care there is a line.

Her father and I keep watch over her,
while her mother boils water for the fever.
Each patient is never far from mind

but this girl here is only four.
How much more must she suffer?
Yesterday I saw two people die.

Sunday Morning

The night seeps back into itself.
The office block across the street
emerges like a coastal shelf,
a forgotten dream revealed.

Meanwhile the light of truth has dawned.
Day awakes. Planes accelerate.
A train makes progress underground.
The hour, the week, the life awaits.

The workplace façade opposite
can now be seen in its detail,
how it was put up brick by brick,
the small efforts that make a wall.

We learn from those who went before
who'll survive metaphorically
to factor in windows, a door,
not retire before work's complete.

Above the river seagulls cry,
going about their bird business,
fishing, mating, knowing to try
is the art of all existence.

Lock-in

After the Tribunal interview
the psychiatrist and I were trapped
in the room as the lock would not unlatch.
And so talk turned to this and that.
It was interesting and therapy in itself
to talk with such a meditative man.
At one point he considered he might climb
out on the balcony and then back in
through another window, but stopped himself
as he thought he might get sectioned too.
He told me about the time he and his wife
got locked out of their Sri Lanka flat,
and him wearing no more than a towel,
how a caretaker climbed down a rope
and let himself onto his balcony.
He told me too of equanimity,
of Averroes and of mindfulness.
He advised nothing more than counselling,
said I had no more than situational stress
and anxiety, and anger at myself
for not having achieved all I had wanted.
Locksmiths came. Eventually the door was
opened with a crowbar and he went on his way.
I have never felt so at ease with a shrink
as when we were both shut in, I think.

A Defence of Blue

To those who ask, 'What is there?',
I say here is sea and air,
a carefully chosen blue,
a meditative, cool hue,

Mediterranean waves
of brushstrokes without a frame,
so the colour overflows
into space. You see I chose

this universal monochrome
so I would feel at peace and home.
Red, yellow, green, black and white
would start rivalries, a fight

of flags' nationalities.
'All is water,' said Thales.
So I conclude, 'All is blue.'
This intent holds its value.

Look further than the pigment
to principle and statement.
Clear your mind. Dive deep into
infinite, subconscious blue.

Stripped of sun, clouds, boats and trees,
this is a silent movie,
or bright ultramarine still
in which nothing is final.

Concert for Anarchy

(after Rebecca Horn)

A grand piano suspended from the ceiling
at intervals performs a high-wire act,
upside-down like a girl's hair hanging
as the swing she is on reaches a crest.

So the lid crashes open and the keys
shoot forth in accompaniment,
with a crescendo of disharmony
in a jangling, discordant movement.

Then the piano calmly reassembles
to repeat its explosive piece,
wresting expression and control
from the romantic composer's genius.

Now imagine an entire orchestra
striking in an empty concert hall,
each instrument starring as its own player
and collective conductor of them all,

the bass jazz of cellos and trombones
in counterpoint to flutes and violins,
ticket office photocopier and telephones,
bar bottles and spotlights joining in.

Hunters

Amid Oxford Street traffic
pedestrians move in herds,
swerving to avoid buses
that bear down like lions

and dodging cyclists
that bolt as if from nowhere,
keen not to be picked off
like wildebeest on the savannah,

or like that beggar,
felled by a can of lager,
lying as if he were a carcass
for hyenas and vultures.

House Martins

Inside the housewife is peeling, cutting, paring,
stirring, boiling, simmering, baking,
sweeping, washing, mopping, polishing,

while outside martins dip and glide:
speeding crescent scythes
too busy to be aware they're alive,

taking insects on the wing, nesting, twittering,
just as her hand swoops to the ironing
and she starts to sing.

Vole

When I was a child,
our dog found a baby vole
in the coal shed,
eyes blind, paws tiny, skin wrinkled.
I took it to the young vet
who lived in our lane
and whom I'd seen
through his cottage window naked.

He fed it milk from a syringe,
then instructed me to leave it
by the entrance to a rabbit hole,
saying the rabbits would take it in.
That night was cold rain.
The next morning at the rabbit hole
I found it dead,
understood cause and effect.

10/10/10

This is the death mask of the year,
the wait before the dawn appears,
the long advent of the solstice,
the day's duress.

This is the apple-storing time,
the season for rake and sowed line,
for planting bulbs as earth hardens
winter wooden.

These are the evenings turned to dark,
the trees undressing to their bark,
the swallows leaving and redwings
now arriving.

Gift

(for Dorothy Wells)

Standing in St Stephen's with St John
as the Last Post called for Remembrance,
I thought of three grandparents now gone
and one left, like a Holy Ghost,
born in '15 as the Great War raged,
then mother of a baby in the Blitz
and of my mother before peace was made,
raised by her own mother as a Baptist.
She still outlives wars we fight today,
battling angina, rheumatism, poor vision.
Each night she prays for me, so I pray
for her heart, like a superstition:
Doris, 'gift of God', may you wake each day
and say, 'I'm still here. I must want to be.'

Give

Old age is when you know all the answers,
but nobody asks you the questions,
when happy memories are plasters
for poverty and isolation,

when you're frightened to go out at night
and by day you worry you'll fall,
when the end of pain's nowhere in sight
and telly's better than watching the wall,

when you've experience to contribute,
but people rush past, or condescend,
when you've travelled the length of the route,
but you don't want to get to the end.

So pick up the phone to your granddad.
Take your grandma out in her chair.
When you think that times are bad,
remember what they have to bear.

They're the last. Their friends have all died.
They've wisdom but no one to tell.
One day you may regret you've not tried.
One day you'll be old as well.

Wish

Just as I was dreaming I was twenty-one,
half a lifetime away with a chance to make right
all the things since then I could have done,
I opened my eyes to midsummer light

imagining a god had granted my wish
to click on a repair date and restore,
and now I am filled with overspilling gladness
that I am forty-two, not eighty-four.

Apples

This is the mother of all Bramleys,
whence came the graft,
or graft of a graft,

that bears the fruit for a pie
made to a grandmother's recipe
for stewed apple and pastry.

'Take a deep well dish,
flour, lard, butter, a pinch
of salt. Mix with your fingertips.'

Now her sight has failed,
she dictates the ritual afters
for a Sunday roast.

And here in Nottinghamshire
this tree, planted as a pip
in the nineteenth century,

almost two centuries on
can still stand and bear
as much fruit as a ton.

Hand-me-downs

My grandmother says her mother said,
'You'll lead a healthy life until you marry,
if you don't do anything
you wouldn't want me to see you doing.'
She says modesty is undervalued
and remembers how her mother cut down
her moleskin coat to make a waist-length jacket,
which she wore with a long rayon scarf
to look like Isadora Duncan,
how she had her hair cut like Clara Bow,
short and straight with a kiss-curl,
which she wore with a crescent hat,
and how her mother exclaimed,
'If you only knew how foolish you look!'

Diamond Jubilee

As if a clock were stuck on Roman numerals
and a history lesson not yet over,
I hear a student playing scales,
then the treble singing of a choir,

and I'm back with the first Elizabethans,
as chalk dust dances in the sun,
and England is lighting beacons
and the Armada about to burn,

instead of in a class teaching poetry
before the Jubilee weekend,
when the thousand prows of a fleet
will sail like victory down the Thames,

and now as trumpet notes join in
with an entrance voluntary,
I picture the meeting of two queens
in an avenue of heraldry

midway on Westminster Bridge,
shaking hands, caught on camera,
then an inaudible exchange
and each walking backwards from the other.

Biology

Let's be pansy and honey bee,
daffodil and bumble,
columbine and butterfly,
dog rose and beetle,

wind and scarlet pimpernel,
the breeze and the poppy,
the bulb and the bluebell,
the root and wild strawberry.

Natural Science

That the way trees breathe is photosynthesis
does not describe summer's glorious green.
That the human body has an epidermis
tells nothing of touch, or the sun, on skin.

That a rose is a means of reproduction
omits its beauty, thorn and scent.
That taste is but a stage in nutrition
misses the cherry's sweetness as we eat.

That mankind evolved on the savannah
caused, but is not, pleasure at seeing for miles.
That the eye is pupil, lens and retina
is less than my sensed image of a smile.

That rain is the water cycle of oceans
forgets just how a cloudy day feels.
That music is soundwaves meeting membranes
loses the soul of Beethoven's symphonies.

That the earth's satellite is formed of rock
cannot catch the awe of a full moon.
That mind and thought are synaptic
is not sufficient to explain what ideas mean.

That the heart is muscle, vein and valve
ignores the wonder when we sense it leap.
That the selfish gene is more precise than love
will never make that one word obsolete.

All Where Each Is

There is a force penetrating every form,
even those that are inanimate,
and this is love,

binding the universe
with patience and laughter,
dawning in togetherness,

when hearts are like summer evenings
and communities gather
like clouds of starlings

preparing to journey over sea,
or like salmon leaping,
making their way upriver

to breed at the place they were born,
flashes of courage and silver,
best viewed after heavy rain.

Freeman

Be glad for the city's spirit, the pulse
that moves the crowd forward, for lives that cross
and pass and meet again, for every face,
her smile, his frown, his singing on the train,
for synagogue and temple, Arab and African,
hospital, school, gallery, museum,
for bars and shops, bus stops, that ambulance,
for work and plans, and what comes by chance
in the hip hop chaos, the quantum dance,
for the knowledge, when we die, London goes on living
beyond rush hour, streetlights, sirens, clubs closing,
to birdsong, planes, road sweepers, the Tube moving
to the end of each line to return once more,
for the coming and going, for the key, the door.

Finding

(for Aidan Williams)

After a difficult week at work,
when I was trying too hard on a short fuse,
I suddenly knew that all the hurt
would have a certain way of being released,

Googled stables in the centre of town
and telephoned, but not to book a ride,
just to have five minutes with any one
of the ponies, and as he fed I cried

deeply from a well I thought was dry,
and while I hugged, breathed fully of his sweat,
heard him intently chomping on the hay,
told him I loved him and kissed his neck,

I knew calm like that with you this afternoon,
my head on your heartbeat, animal and true.

Flying

As the plane took off with me in dual control,
the best bit was looking back and seeing you
smiling, excited, saying 'linga linga lu',
your morning shower song of a happy soul,

and as I steered alone, nose up and down,
I thought of my mother and me inside her,
like Russian dolls, leaving New York and America
for the landing of my birth in London,

and I realised my effect on you the passenger
as I dived and deliberately caused turbulence,
just as I had been talkative and nervous
on arrival at the aerodrome and hangar,

and thinking I'd like to deliver us children,
I saw the need for balance and for calm,
for attaining the meditation of concentration
when flying and attempting the unknown.

Beyond the Fallacy of Nought

Is nought a fallacy and illusion,
created by mathematics and religion,
and does and did the void not exist,
since there was no start to spark physics,
no nothing at all that lit the big bang,
and from that double negative sang
and sings there, not a fire, or wind on a sea,
but the counterpoint of eternity,
the epic metre of the universe,
which is, was ever, a poem, never formless,
has and had no ending, nor beginning,
no boundaries, but kept and keeps on singing,
just as midnight is not the zero hour,
and emptiness contains the container,
and there is, was never, nothing in between
the entities of one and minus one,
the heart of the matter and anti-matter,
for the entire world is a prime number,
and as such is and was indivisible
and endless as a curve with infinite numerals,
and though there is consequence and collision,
the existence of the space-time continuum
cancels out cause and explanation,
so that there is no blank in calculation,
and though in language and maths there are signs,
in reality there are no reasons, just rhymes,
pairs of positive and negative charges,
that generate and generated mass down ages,
with the result that there is force of argument,
yet is, was not, nor will be, a decimal point,
only fractions *versus* units, tens, hundreds,
a balance of consonance and assonance,
the whole system as gloriously stable
as eggs and flour on kitchen scales?